CW00429434

# Read*ux*

Readux Books: Series 5, No 17

ISBN: 978-3-944801-31-5

Cover by Adeline Meilliez
Design by Susann Stefanizen

Published by Readux Books
Sorauer Str. 16, 10997 Berlin, Germany

www.readux.net

# The Idea of a River
*Walking out of Berlin*

*Paul Scraton*

*"A solitary walker, however short his or her route, is unsettled, between places, drawn forth into action by desire and lack, having the detachment of the traveler rather than the ties of the worker, the dweller, the member of a group."*

—*Rebecca Solnit*

It is seven o'clock in the morning and I'm starting at the end, at the point where the Panke river is swallowed whole by the Berlin-Spandau Ship Canal. It has concluded its thirty-two kilometre journey from its source right where I'm going to begin my walk. Not that I'm quite ready to start, enjoying as I am this solitude in the heart of the city. And then I realise that I'm not quite alone.

The fisherman sits on a squat stool, rod resting on a stand between his legs, his hat pulled low over his head. He looks at peace, eyes cast forward across the calm waters of the canal, his thermos flask of coffee on one side, a cool box filled with supplies on the other. I can see him an hour or so earlier, stepping out from his nearby apartment, walking along the river to his regular patch on the canal bank. He's been coming here for years, since a time when no-one came to this corner of the city, when the neighbourhood was enclosed by the Wall and he could feel the eyes of the East German border guards on his back. Now they have built

5

townhouses in the death strip, laid a new bike path along the embankment, and landscaped the verges. Back in the eighties our fisherman would stay long into the night, losing track of time on a summer's evening until they turned on the floodlights in the no-man's land. That would be the hint it was time to pack up and head to the pub on the corner of his street.

He used to have the canal bank to himself. Now, on a sunny day, he shares it with Turkish families and their barbecues, students with their bicycles and the books that lie at their side, mostly unread. Tour guides tell stories about the Wall in a multitude of languages. Back then, when he walked home along the Panke he would cross a Chausseestraße empty of traffic, basically a dead-end street leading down to the checkpoint at the Wall. Now it streams with traffic, day and night, the old post road to Hamburg busy again, and he has to wait for a gap to get across.

Are all these changes for the better? His opinion shifts with his mood. As long as he comes early he always gets his spot. The families don't bother him, and neither do the students. The factory where he used to work has been turned into a bar, and the pub on the corner of his street has been closed and boarded up for two years. He likes that the riverside path has been tidied up, that old folks sit on benches and kids play beneath the weeping willow trees. Some old faces have gone, replaced by newcomers – like those in the townhouses. But places change, and he was a newcomer once.

The fisherman picks up his coffee and takes a careful sip. He winces, and blows gently into the little hole in the lid. I am suddenly aware of the cold in my fingers and toes. I need to get moving. It's going to be a long day.

*

Almost from the first step I lose the river as it disappears beneath an open-air ice rink, abandoned for the season. To pick it up again I skirt a collection of football pitches and tennis courts, a sports complex built for the employees of a pharmaceutical company that has been working out of this corner of Berlin for over a hundred and fifty years. The river has re-emerged beside the car park, but I don't see it again until the other side of Chausseestraße, where it passes through an apartment block that has been built on either side of and above the water to form an arch. The new townhouses and the shiny German automobiles parked in front of them are still within sight… and yet here, on the other side of the old East-West divide, it feels like a world away. A hundred balconies house a hundred satellite dishes, maintaining connection to a homeland far away. Turkey, Serbia, Portugal and Lebanon. Morocco, Russia, Croatia and Poland. Since the 1960s this has been an immigrant neighbourhood, and it remains that way.

At this time of day, the path along the river is quiet. In an hour or so the commuter rush will come, the cyclists whizzing through from the suburbs in the north to the offices in the city centre. They pass through the district of Wedding with barely a pause, part of their everyday route to and from work. And I am the same, albeit a little slower, for this is where I have made my home, and so I barely take note any more of the cityscape as I walk through it each day. But not today. Today I am walking with my eyes raised.

I estimate the age of the buildings that line the canal bank. 1950s. 1980s. Last year. A building site. Very little of prewar industrial Wedding remains, a neighbourhood transformed by bombs and the post-War division of the city. Surviving factories have become dance studios and artists' workshops. I walk past a piano-builders' in an old bus depot, and a warehouse offering bonsai trees. The streets that cross the river are lined with slot machine-filled 'casinos', internet cafes offering phone cards to every conceivable country in the world, and euro-stores piled high with plastic toys, toilet brushes and Tupperware boxes. But mostly I'm walking through the neighbourhood alongside the river under a canopy of trees, a world away from the popular perception of poverty and crime that lingers in the imagination of those who never spend any time here.

Within sight of my apartment building, I make my way into the Soldiner Kiez, a neighbourhood that carries a reputation for abandoned shop fronts and a local mob collecting protection money from second-hand clothing stores and kebab stands. But times change quicker than reputations, familiarity breeds security, and many of those empty properties now house pop-up art galleries and studio spaces. The local kids walking the river path on their way to school are well-scrubbed and cheerful, and if the pub on the corner is already doing a roaring trade with the early drinkers who have spilled out onto the pavement, beer glasses in hand, they are joined in the tableau before me by a slim jogger, her feet dancing lightly between the scattered glass of a broken beer bottle.

The buildings retreat around an overflow basin, filled not with water but weeds and tall grasses.

With the tower blocks to the back of the scene, the sky opens up. On the opposite bank are the first allotment gardens of my walk; a colony of cabins surrounded by neatly-mown lawns and flags celebrating everything from Wedding, Berlin and Germany, to the heroes of the Hertha BSC football club and the Ferrari Formula One racing team. As I pass a couple of thuggish-looking guys and their equally thuggish-looking dogs, I can feel myself being watched. Across the river a man leans on his fence, taking a break from shovelling leaves onto the bonfire that burns gently behind him. I catch his eye and offer up a smile but his expression doesn't change.

And then, a few steps further, no longer in view of grumpy allotment holders, past a red brick factory and plastic football pitch and I'm crossing the old border once more, this time beneath the railway lines of the north-south S-Bahn. I emerge from the tunnel and into leafy Pankow, an East Berlin neighbourhood where the streets have shaken off the sleep of socialist hibernation and are now lined with organic supermarkets, toy shops filled with hand-crafted wooden playthings, and cafes where children are encouraged to run riot as their well-dressed parents sip on Third Wave Coffee and flick through the pages of *Die Zeit*, *TAZ* or the *Frankfurter Allgemeine*.

*

This is a neighbourhood of would-be kings, and not only the little princes who run amok in the *Kindercafe*. For a time Otto Witte lived on Wollankstraße, close to the border with Pankow and not far from the banks of the Panke. Witte was born in 1871, the year of the first German unification, and grew up in a travelling family of circus entertainers to become an illiterate showman who tamed lions and swallowed fire.

A life performing to provincial German crowds in a big top was not enough for Otto, and so he took himself out into the world to embark on a story that would resonate so long that it is still being told in Berlin's *Tagesspiegel* newspaper a hundred years later. In his twenties Otto Witte landed in Abyssinia, inveigling his way into the inner circle of the royal court before eloping with the Emperor's fourteen-year-old daughter. The couple were captured on the coast, and Otto was sentenced to death, but among his many skills was escape artistry, and he beat a hasty retreat from the Horn of Africa. Always on the move, he explored South America, spent time in London and Cairo and worked as a hunter in Kenya and a tour guide in the Holy Land. He joined the Foreign Legion and then absconded when he realised how strenuous the training was. He became a pearl diver in the Mediterranean and befriended Lenin in Switzerland.

He eventually arrived in Constantinople, where he joined the Ottoman army, before becoming a spy for the secret service. At this time Albania was in the process of breaking free from the Empire, and was looking for a new leader. They decided upon Prince Halim, a nephew of the Sultan, and made arrangements to offer him the crown. Otto knew that he looked like the prince, and so he hatched a plot, travelling first to Vienna to fit himself out in a suitable disguise before heading south to claim the throne.

The rule of King Otto would last five days, long enough to appoint his best friend to the position of minister, plan war with Montenegro and select eleven daughters of Albania for his harem, before the real Prince Halim got wind of what was going on and sent word to Albania that they had crowned an imposter. Once again he was forced to retreat, emptying the reserves of the treasury before catching a fishing boat to Italy. It was after this particular escapade that he made his way to Berlin, and an apartment on Wollankstraße, just a short walk from the *Bürgerpark*.

I ponder Otto Witte's story as I walk through the park, along red gravel paths that stain the soles of my shoes as I pass the bandstand and reach the beer garden. The beer garden is not open yet, but I take a break and sit down at one of its white painted tables. On the open expanse of grass a small group of young men and women stretch, following the instructions of a shaven-headed instructor. A toddler kicks a football, unsteady on his feet. A great tit calls from the tree above my head. It sounds like a bicycle pump.

Otto didn't ease up on his adventures once he lived in Berlin, founding a political party in the middle of the Weimar-era turmoil and keeping the 'Former King of Albania' on his business card until the end of his life. He died in Hamburg, where he was buried with the title safely chiselled into his gravestone for eternity. But there is one problem with this story: there is no evidence to prove that it is true. 'I had sincerely hoped to bring peace and happiness to Albania,' he told Australian newspaper *The Age*, late in his life. He always stuck to his story.

I leave the park and follow the Panke through some leafy streets of Wilhelmine apartment buildings until I reach the grounds of an actual royal palace. For all the stories of Prussian Kings navigating the shallow waters of the Panke from Charlottenburg to Pankow, the reality is that this palace and the nearby villa colony built on the other side of the river owe their fame to another group of would-be kings, in the post-War German Democratic Republic. The Schönhausen Palace was the first official residence of GDR President Wilhelm Pieck, and later became a governmental guesthouse. The villas themselves were home to the other leading members of the Politburo, who gathered there in the late 1940s in a fenced-in compound following the founding of communist East Germany.

It was from these villas that the likes of Pieck, General Secretary Walter Ulbricht, and the rest of the motley group hid from the throngs of disgruntled workers during the 1953 Uprising, when order was restored thanks only to Soviet tanks. Three years and some events in Hungary would persuade the East German leadership that it was possible to live too close to the people in whose name they were governing, and they skedaddled north to a fortified complex in Wandlitz.

There, as in Pankow – with the Panke flowing gently at the bottom of some of their gardens – this unelected group of socialist 'royalty' lived in close proximity to one another; the Ulbrichts observing the Honeckers over the backyard fence. Later, in the forests of Brandenburg, this intimacy would become unbearable for many, leaving members of the Politburo and their spouses to complain that it was like living in a particularly well-appointed prison, a complaint of many members of royal families over the years.

They are all gone now. Real kings and fake kings, rulers by the grace of God or by Stalin... but their ghosts follow me through Pankow as I go.

\*

I share the neat paths of the palace grounds with a good number of dogs, runners and cyclists, only some of whom wear neon Lycra, but all are getting their morning exercise. At the far end I reach a complex of GDR-era *Plattenbauten*, those prefabricated housing blocks found all across the former East, and have to pause at a traffic light that will help me cross a busy road. This marks the edge of the city proper, and I'm moving now into the liminal zone, a ten kilometre stretch that is neither city nor country, a place of suburban housing estates nudging up against edgeland spaces; the sewage works and the motorway slip road, the allotment gardens and the industrial parks, the golf clubs and the logistics warehouses.

The path follows its bank through a tunnel of trees, the autobahn rumbles behind a high wall to my right as it leads out from the city to the ring motorway that surrounds Berlin. To my left, through a tangle of branches and some wire fencing I can see some office workers from the business park taking a cigarette break outside the door of their building. They could be in an office supplies company on the edge of Manchester. An online auction house on the fringe of Newark. An insurance call centre on the outskirts of Paris. I watch them for a while, camouflaged by the trees, until, cigarettes finished, they re-enter the building and climb the stairs to their open-plan office, to the whir of desk fans and the grinding and flickered flash of light from a photocopier in almost constant use.

For the next hour I walk through these edgelands, the path taking me past carp ponds and some more late morning fishermen, tranquil on their stools despite the continuous roar of the motorway. At one point the path takes me over the stream of traffic – the river passing beneath. I stand on the footbridge mesmerised by the speed, and have to move on before the dizziness has me toppling forward into the flow of cars and trucks racing below.

A sandy path runs between allotment gardens, and I kick the dirt with my shoes, listening for snippets of conversation and the bark of suspicious dogs. A woman eyes me warily as I approach. This is obviously not a stretch of the footpath much used by those who don't have business here. I smile and offer a greeting. Perhaps it is hearing my accent that causes her to visibly relax, as if my foreignness can explain my out-of-place presence, and she offers a 'good morning' of her own.

More allotments and rusting garages, and then I reach the ponds, built in the nineteenth century as part of the network of sewage fields developed to deal with the waste of the millions of new Berliners, like Otto Witte, who found themselves drawn to the German capital as it became the Metropolis of the 1920s. These fields ringed the city, allowing nature to filter the waste. They were so ingenious that they were still used until just before the fall of the Berlin Wall, when they finally reached the end of their service life and were returned to nature.

In Karow I experience the sewage fields as a series of wildflower-filled meadows above which butterflies dance. I share the path with birdwatchers now, lugging their equipment alongside the river to find a hidden spot by the ponds. If you did not know the history of the place you would presume you had finally left Berlin behind and reached the countryside. But it isn't, not really. This is a product of industrialisation as much as the streets around my apartment building in Wedding, and the old factories that have become dance studios. The ponds, like the factories, have simply found another use.

After the ponds I'm faced once more with a foot-bridge over the motorway. And this time it is the Berliner Ring. It feels like I am crossing a boundary, as if the Panke has finally led me out of the city. Officially this is not true, and if I had a map I would know that there is still quite a lot of 'Berlin' left to walk through. But as I drop down from the bridge I see the first ploughed fields of my walk, and in any case, I am simply following the river. I didn't bring a map.

\*

Strolling alongside that field, I feel incredibly small as I pass underneath the slung wires hanging from enormous electricity pylons. I am two thirds of the way there, all those kilometres covered before lunchtime, and my feet are beginning to protest. The Panke is still there but so too is the railway line. Although I have not seen it up to now, my route along the river has been followed at a greater and lesser distance by the S-Bahn that, like the Panke, starts and ends its journey in the small town of Bernau beyond the city limits. To find the source of the river that flows past my apartment I could have taken the train... door to door in half an hour.

I am approaching the suburb of Buch and I can see the S-Bahn sign tempting me from the path. I could climb those steps and complete the journey in a matter of minutes. Who would know?

Ting-ting!

I step aside, stumbling slightly on the uneven verge. Two cyclists pass, whizzing along at speed, their panniers matching their skin-tight shirts, a map resting on a handlebar bag below the lead rider's nose. To Bernau or beyond? The path along the Panke is part of a much longer bike route, from Berlin to the Baltic Sea. That would have been another option. Borrow a bike. Ride to Bernau. Back home for lunch.

Despite my aching feet, I know that this is the way that I want to do this. In her marvellous history of walking, Rebecca Solnit argues that the mind works best at three miles an hour, a proposition with which the French philosopher Frédéric Gros agrees: 'When you are walking, nothing moves: only imperceptibly do the hills draw closer, the surroundings change.' They are both right. Those cyclists, already past the station and beyond, may see the colourful flash of a jay as it swings across the path in front of them, but not the snail resting on the edge of the tarmac. And perhaps they can, like me, read the change in football loyalties as

19

spraycanned on the walls and the motorway bridges of this part of the city, but if they concentrate too hard at speed as to whether we are in Hertha, Union or Galatasaray territory, they may find themselves riding into a tree.

Walks can, in the words of Robert Macfarlane, 'take their bearings from the distant past, but also from the debris and phenomena of the present, for this is often a double insistence of old landscapes: that they be read in the then but felt in the now.' Do the commuters of Brandenburg see this through the smeared carriage windows as their S-Bahn races south on a workday morning to the city?

Perhaps their minds are on other things: the meeting at 9:30 and the lunchtime telephone call; the newspaper app on the phone in front of them; the schoolgirl conversation taking place in the seats behind. From the window they can see the ponds and the back gardens, the supermarkets and the motorway. They can see me, bending down to poke at a snail, before searching out my notebook from my back pocket to record this thought. But who knows if any of this registers? At Buch station I stop, eat a sandwich, and ignore the siren call of the platform. The sign beside the railway bridge tells me Bernau is ten kilometres away. Just a couple of hours more.

*

From bright sunshine into half-light beneath the trees. I have stumbled into a place that feels strange and uncomfortable. The path has led me from the collection of shops around the station and into the *Schlosspark*. These are palace grounds without a palace, for it was destroyed in the 1960s, and although somewhere in the vicinity should be the carefully manicured gardens you would expect, the path alongside the river snakes through tangled bushes and trees, muddy in places with roots lurking to trip the unsuspecting stroller, the air under the woodland canopy dank and heavy.

Mosquitoes buzz, and I quicken my step. At the entrance to the park a couple of workmen shovelled gently rotting leaves into the back of a truck, but now I have the place to myself. I feel uneasy, with no view of the sky. A couple of pathways lead off towards some other corner of the park but both are blocked with metal fences, hastily constructed. I see glimpses of what might be people or could also be stone statues, strangled by the undergrowth. When I had planned this walk I had thought the palace grounds would be a place to break, stretch out on the grass and rest my legs, but it is all too forbidding.

A movement through the trees catches my eye. There, on another path (how do you reach it?), a man in a hospital gown walks slowly, pulling a drip that is hanging from a wheeled contraption. He is walking with a friend – she does not look like a nurse – and they are deep in conversation. It should not be a surprise. Buch was developed over a hundred years ago as the largest 'hospital city' in Europe, and it remains a place of medicine and scientific research. The red brick buildings of the former mental asylum, now part of the hospital, are just a short walk away. I have been there, once, stalking the grounds beneath ivy framed windows as I waited for my daughter to wake up after an operation. The main hospital building is new, but she was being worked on in part of the old asylum, that in turn reminded me of a windswept English public school on the Irish Sea coast where I once went to play a game of hockey.

Did we win the game? Lost in thought I nearly trip over a stray branch that has fallen across my path, and when I look up again, the patient and his companion have disappeared.

I made some notes before the walk. Things to look out for along the way. Curious facts I might wish to confirm, should there be a handily placed expert waiting along the route. Under BUCH

– underlined twice – I had scribbled a handful of words in my notebook.

*Hospitals. Lotte's operation. TB Sanatorium x2. Mental Asylum and Old People's Home. Rest in the Park?*

And then:

*8th May 1945. Buch medical facilities under the Sov. Military Command. Positive ID of burned bodies of A. Hitler and E. Braun. Dental records?*

A sudden crack of branch, and the hurried flap of wings of a too-heavy but unseen bird, cause me jump and to quicken my step further. I've had enough of this place…

…and then, with a turn of the corner, I am out and across a road and I'm walking along a suburban street of neat detached houses on one side and a wheat field on the other. A man in a waxed jacket throws a stick for his dog. A mother leans on her pushchair as she has a conversation with a neighbour over the front gate. The post van is parked at the bottom of the path, the uniformed driver rifling through a collection of plastic-wrapped junk mail to find an actual letter. At some point after emerging from the park I've lost the Panke, but a waymarker stuck to a lamppost tells me I am still heading in the right direction, and I'm just happy to be out in the sunshine once more.

The path leaves the houses behind and crosses the field. Someone has left a message, painted in light blue on the tarmac:

*Bitte*
*verzeihe*
*mir M…*
*Ich werde*
*alles besser*
*Machen.*

The handwriting is large, filling the path, but whoever it is that is making this plaintive cry has neat and proper joined-up writing, only slightly damped by the little flower that has been used to punctuate the last line. I try to picture M. Boy or a girl? I imagine it is a young man, who rides this route to and from his high school. The writer knows M will see the message. If only he can forgive her then she will make it all right.

The field is all grass now, dotted with hay bales. I leave the message for M behind and press on. I have not seen the river for almost twenty minutes now, although I know where it is thanks to a line of trees at the eastern fringe of the fields. At the bottom of the field, where the path reaches a collection of houses once more, I have finally arrived at the limit of Berlin. Just before I come to the first house, and hear the splash of a swimming pool hidden behind a neatly trimmed hedge, I step from the path onto a pavement, and into Brandenburg.

*

The Panke and its path, not always together, wind their way through a collection of communities, strung out from Buch along the S-Bahn line to Bernau. Röntgenthal, named for the inventor of the X-ray. Zepernick, from the Slavic word for dense shrubbery. Friedenstal, the peaceful valley. And Bernau, the end of the line. On this weekday morning these are empty streets I am walking through, with barely a car passing me by. Every so often I come across the river, staring down from a bridge at what is little more than a narrow stream, a ditch even. This area is known as the Panketal – the Panke Valley – but at this point it is more an idea of a river than a proper waterway.

The houses are neat and tidy, with threatening signs involving dogs on the gateposts. German flags fly from a couple of lawns. Outside the train stations hundreds of bicycles are piled up, waiting for their owners to return on the S-Bahn at the end of the working day. Passing beneath yet another motorway, the industrial parks on the outskirts of Bernau come into view. This has been my aim all along and yet I have not given this town at the end of my journey any more than a moment's thought.

A few more fields now. A trout farm and a car showroom. More allotment gardens. More people as well, jogging and cycling and walking their dogs. This river flows for thirty-two kilometres and, so early in its journey and so late in mine, is almost completely swallowed by the thick patch of nettles growing on either bank. When I get to Bernau I will head to the Devil's Pool, a pond around the back of a shopping centre – supposedly one source of the Panke – and then down a side street at the edge of town to a patch of soggy marshland that is possibly the other. The Panke does not emerge from the ground in any dramatic form, bursting through limestone from an underground cave or into a great lake of the region. It just seeps onto the surface. Having walked out from the city, it just seems to disappear. There is nothing left to mark the end of this journey.

Does it matter? Not really. If I had wanted the Panke to lead me somewhere, I would have walked in the other direction.

At an *Imbiss* outside the station I buy a beer, sit down on a bench, and drink a toast to the Panke. And then I catch the S-Bahn home.

## Works Cited

Otto Witte quoted in Borck, Werner. 'King of Albania for Five Days'. Melbourne: *The Age Newspaper*, 28 January 1959.

Gros, Frédéric. *The Philosophy of Walking*. London: Verso, 2014.

Macfarlene, Robert. *The Old Ways: A Journey on Foot*. London: Hamish Hamilton, 2012.

Solnit, Rebecca. *Wanderlust: A History of Walking*. London: Verso, 2001.

Zander, Ulrich. 'Berlins gekrönter König'. Berlin: *Tagesspiegel Newspaper*, 2 February 2013.

## Paul Scraton

Born just outside Liverpool, Paul Scraton moved to Berlin in 2001. He is the founder and editor of the Under a Grey Sky website, devoted to 'adventures beyond the front door' and has spent the past couple of years exploring the Berlin Wall Trail for his project Traces of a Border. He has written for *The Guardian*, *Hidden Europe*, Slow Travel Berlin and Caught by the River, runs neighbourhood walking tours in Berlin, and is the editor in chief of *Elsewhere: A Journal of Place*, a quarterly print publication launched in 2015.